I0465715

The Reporting Revolution
2nd Edition

Because reporting should be more
than checking a box.

Written & Illustrated
by Chris Lysy

1st Edition: August 31, 2022
2nd Edition: November 11, 2025

For the amazing women in my life;
Jen, Mady, Sue, & Lesley.

For Henry & Kevin, whose support is
still felt.

And for the researchers and evaluators
who do work far too important for it
to just fade into obscurity.

The Reporting Revolution

Introduction
A Little Story

Do you know the story of Cassandra? It goes something like this...

Girl meets a god who gives her a divine power to see the future. The girl then turns down the god's romantic advances. The god, who is clearly a creepy jerk, feels scorned and curses the girl. The girl can still see the future (her gift) but nobody will believe her prophecies (her curse).

We researchers and evaluators also have a gift. We can't see the future, but through our methods we can measure the past and monitor the present. Then we can use that knowledge to project the future.

And like Cassandra we also have a curse. There is no guarantee that anyone will hear our words or believe what we share.

But unlike Cassandra, our curse is at least partially self-inflicted. We use the web to share our work in much the same way as we did in the late 90s. And we write reports almost as if the last 20 years never happened.

I believe we need a change, a monumental change. Not necessarily in our tools but in our mindsets.

Because the status quo is a path towards irrelevance.

This is me.

I wrote this book to be a practical guide for an alternative approach to reporting. It's based on my real world experiences as a researcher, evaluator, and information designer over the last two decades.

Here is what you'll learn:

- In chapter 1 you'll learn why I think a change in our reporting approach is necessary.

- In chapter 2 you'll learn how to identify and segment your reporting audiences.

- In chapter 3 you'll learn how to think about and build a modern digital reporting strategy.

- In chapter 4 you'll learn how to develop an efficient and effective report design system.

- In chapter 5 I give you a simple call to action.

Note: This book is self-published and written informally. It's filled with contractions, silly pictures, and possibly some typos. It will feel a lot like a really long blog post and not so much like a textbook.

Originally published in the summer of 2022. This current edition was updated in fall of 2025.

What's new:

- It's black & white. That makes it cheaper to print and lets me bring the price way down.

- The book is now 6x9, because I like it when text has breathing room.

- I've added new illustrations and made a few tweaks.

Chapter 1
The BIG Why

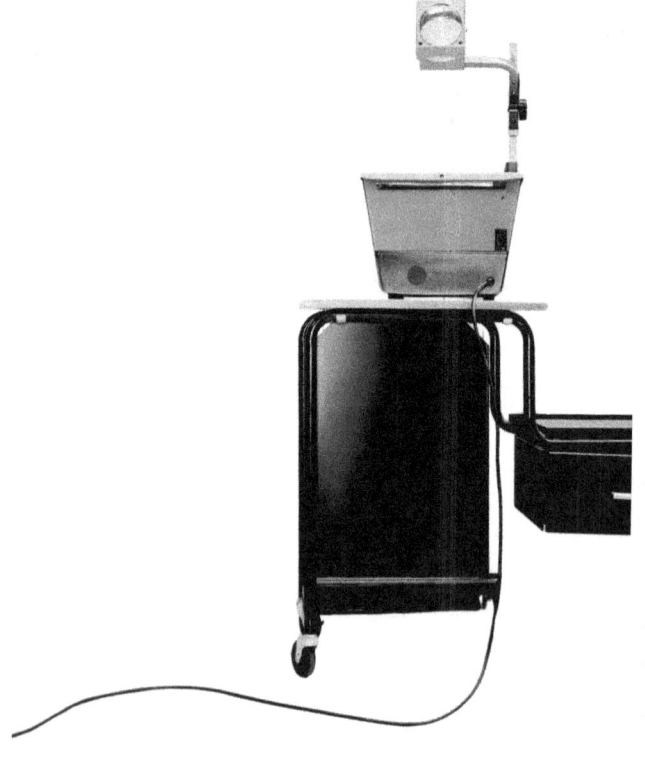

Why are we still reporting like it's 1999?

So back in 1999, if you wanted to share a report, you would either create an html version of the report or share a downloadable PDF.

Flash forward to ~~2022~~ 2025. Now if you want to share a report, most organizations will either create an html version of the report or share a downloadable PDF.

It's almost as if the last couple of decades never happened. Let's see what we've missed:

- Social Media. For instance, Twitter and Facebook didn't exist until the 2000s. In 1999, Mark Zuckerberg was still in high school.

- Smart Phones and Flat Screen Monitors. The range of screen sizes you have in your home is incredibly wide compared to 1999.

- UX Design as a Web Design Paradigm. User experience design predates 1999, but it did not have anywhere near the reputation it has nowadays.

- Big Data and Easy Access Analytics. Google Analytics didn't launch until 2005, lots of websites still had hit counters in 1999.

- Easier to Use Reporting Tools. Back in 1999 you had Word and PowerPoint. Now we also have fun things like Canva and Wordpress.

It's not that the reporting approach from 1999 is bad. PDFs still might be the way to go, sometimes. But we can do better than just a long PDF on a resource site, we have the technology.

*Note from 2025 Chris: I'm working on a new book right now called, "The PDF Must Die." Let's just say, I have a less nuanced opinion these days about reporting with a PDF.

freshspectrum

Our reports tell everyone else a story about our profession.

They tell everyone that our profession is stuck in the old days. We're behind the times and out of touch.

Are they wrong?

In the first decade of the 2000s, the newspaper industry started a rapid decline. Newsrooms were closed, reporters lost their jobs, and business models were turned upside down. This collapse kicked off a transformation that is still ongoing.

But the market forces that toppled the newspaper industry didn't topple the research and evaluation industry. We have never needed to rely on advertising and print circulation. While most of our money comes from public and nonprofit institutions, and many of us see our roles as serving the public good, our work rarely serves the public directly.

So we haven't felt the same economic pressure to transform as other industries. We deliver what our funders expect us to deliver. We then leave the sharing to their communications teams and move on to new projects.

Our biggest reporting challenge is not rapidly changing technology but an established status quo that expects too little.

Seeing our work through our audience's eyes.

When you ask an evaluation team to explain their report's audience, what do they say?

Do they mention clients, program staff, other evaluators, other researchers, board members, teachers, program administrators, politicians, and the "general public?"

Eye roll.

It's not that those are bad audiences to try to reach. It's just that you can rarely reach any audience with just one PDF report. Most likely you are just writing that one report for yourselves and the people paying your bills. Somebody else might read it, but be honest, was it really written for them?

Nobody wakes up in the morning, gets a cup of coffee and thinks, "you know what I'm going to do, I'm going to scroll through an online archive of PDF evaluation reports."

Think about the individuals in your audience. Every person has their own quirks and motivations. Pick one and look at your work through their eyes.

What do you see? If you were one of these people, would you even know your work exists?

If you do end up finding a report, how would you go about reading it? Would you sit down, open up your computer and read the PDF from start to finish? Or would you just skim your way through?

It's not the quality of the one report that's the problem. But our expectations that the one report serves all the people we would like to serve.

Unintentional gatekeepers.

Your work is interesting.

If it wasn't, why would you or anybody else be doing it? Why would anybody put funding towards it?

The further we get into a topic, the more we lose sight of what made it interesting in the first place. We start to overthink it and decide that we need more time to share what we've learned. And then we spend a ton of time putting together our thoughts.

Eventually we end up with one longish report that gets shared very little.

We could make excuses and blame the audience. But were you there for them when they needed you? Maybe you have the specific answers to their questions but didn't include them in the report.

The more we learn, the more we have to share. And if we don't actively share what we've learned, we become gatekeepers.

freshspectrum

Mindset Change - Report as a Product to Reporting as a Process.

It's time to stop thinking about a report as a solitary thing. Instead of thinking about THE report. Part of problem is that we treat a report like a product.

The product form of a report is annual or at the end of the project. It's that one thing you deliver before you move on with your other work.

The process of reporting is an ongoing conversation you have with different audiences. It doesn't have to be a PDF. You could report through a series of emails, blog posts, infographics, tweets, YouTube videos, or Zoom calls.

When you think of reporting as a process, it should change how you approach reporting in general. Since we are not focused on delivering one thing, the emphasis should be on ways that we can reach our audience on a regular basis.

This is what we miss when we treat our report like a product. It assumes that someone else is connected to the audience that wants or needs access to our work. It also assumes that the someone else is going to care enough about our work to share it with that audience. These are bad assumptions. Engagement is hard, and it's even harder when sharing second hand data.

If we really want to effectively report our work, we need all the things that it takes to do that. Things like landing pages, email lists, featured images, and social media accounts. We also need to listen, not just shout.

This dashboard is
a solid first step.
Can the project team
suggest a few tweaks?

No, we could
barely afford the
initial development.

freshspectrum.com

Not just better, faster too.

Trying to improve the quality of your reports is a worthwhile pursuit. At first it might take you more time to create better work. You might even come to the conclusion that good things just take time. But it doesn't have to take more time.

Most researchers and evaluators already spend a lot of time reporting, even when the reports are ugly and boring. The actual problem is that we spend a lot of time on inconsequential things.

We go back and forth wordsmithing phrases in paragraphs that will hardly ever be read. We spend time tweaking table formats in Word, even when the report is eventually going to be redesigned by somebody else. We write a hundred pages even when there is a 50 page limit.

Realistically, we are not going to be given more time to do better work. So we just need to create better work in less time.

Luckily there are ways to do that, by creating your own design systems, writing style guides, building asset libraries, and developing templates.

Because the thing that will make you and your work more valuable is being able to do better work in less time.

I got an idea. Let's spend our entire reporting budget creating a document that will only be read by the few people who feel obligated to do so.

freshspectrum

Make it easy.

Which is better, one amazing report OR ten pretty good reports?

Actually, let's rephrase that. Which is better, reaching a small portion of your audience with one amazing report, while leaving the bulk of your audience with next to nothing OR reaching 10 different portions of your audience, each one with a pretty good report designed just for them?

If you only have one audience and plenty of time you can shoot for amazing. But for the rest of us, good enough is good enough.

It's okay if the infographic is formulaic and built from a widely used template. It's okay if that visual slidedoc only took you an afternoon to create. Your audience will not care.

So don't overthink it.

Use the tools that are the easiest to learn.

Create the way you know how to create.

Make it as easy as possible.

Then repeat.

It's up to you.

The status quo is powerful.

But if you want to take it down, you can take it down.

It might not be easy, but it is possible with a little hard work and a lot of dedication.

Chapter 2
Finding Your Audience

Dr. Frankenstein's Audience

— Board Member
— Scholar
— Program Participant
— Parent
— Staff Member
— Funder

Default Audience Avatar

freshspectrum

Who is in your audience?

First question, who is in your audience?

Now for a few follow-ups:

- Are they really in your audience?
- Do you have a way to reach these people?
- Will they actually hear what you have to say?

A theoretical audience is not an audience. Listing types of people that may or may not have the potential to be interested in what you have to say, is not an audience.

Real audiences are tangible. They are the people standing in the auditorium when you walk up to the podium. They are the list of 300 email addresses collected from past program participants. They are the unique pageviews that show up in Google Analytics.

Live in a room (and sometimes in a webinar) we get to see real live people. But even digital audiences that visit your website leave some kind of trace. If you look, there is always at least some evidence when an audience exists.

Unfortunately we rarely look. Maybe because we already know what we would find, or rather, not find.

In order to report in the modern world, you first need access to a real audience. And if you don't have access to a real audience, you either need to borrow an audience or spend some time building one.

Activity: Naming your Audience

Often when we discuss our audience we talk through the generic groups of people we want to reach. But I don't want you to do that kind of naming.

Think about the audience for something you've written in the past. It could be a report, a blog post, a journal article, or pretty much anything else.

Now try to name 5 people who read that thing.
Their actual names.

If 5 was easy, try to name 10 people or 20 people.

If 5 was hard, just try to name 1 or 2.

When we come up with generic audience groupings our audiences become fiction. Real audience members are human beings with names, personality traits, preferences, needs, and quirks. The more that you can picture the real people in your audience, the better your reporting.

Your Big 3 Audiences

So every person in your audience is unique. But unless you have unlimited time, you can't tailor your report format for every single person.

In the evaluation world there is an often shared reporting convention that can be traced back to a 2001 brief by the Canadian Health Services Research Foundation. It goes something like this, "1 page brief, 3 page executive summary, 25 page report."

It's not a bad convention, each of the three report types appeal to people with different levels of interest. But let's take that idea one step further. Instead of sticking to prescribed page lengths let's think about the audience that each report type is designed to serve.

Who is your 25 page report audience?

This is likely your client, boss, or whomever commissioned your work. It might also be really engaged program staff or other stakeholders who have a high level of interest in your work.

In the digital world, these are the people who subscribe to your newsletter and regularly read most things you share.

Who is your 3 page executive summary audience?

These are the people who feel compelled to read your work, but don't want 25 pages. They might be non-profit board members, partners, and other people who have a medium interest in your work.

In the digital world, these are the people who follow you from a distance on social media. Sometimes they read what you share, or like what you post, but only if it shows up in their feed.

Who is your 1 page audience?

These are people who might not know much about your work and just have a casual interest. It could also be the audiences that are only interested in one very small piece of your work.

In the digital world, these are the people who find something you have shared through Google. Or perhaps they have seen one of your social media posts through a friend's retweet or through a hashtag they follow.

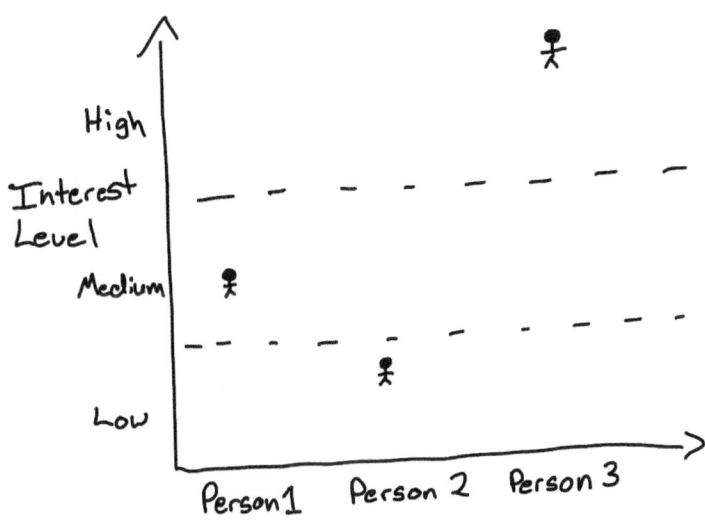

Activity: Three Bucket Audience

Go back to people you picked in the audience naming activity or choose a small group of individuals that might be interested in a report you hope to share in the future.

Classify each person by the interest level they would have in your work. And be honest, just because you wish your client or boss would be very interested in the report you are writing does not make it so.

The three buckets are:
- Low Interest (i.e. your 1 pager crowd)
- Medium Interest (i.e. your executive summary crowd)
- High Interest (i.e. your full report crowd)

34

When I was your age, we presented in front of real people. We could see their eyes and hear their voices. If our presentation was bad, we knew it.

freshspectrum

The Audience Growth Saturation Point

Do you have a close-ended or an open-ended audience? In other words, is your audience limited to a specific number of individuals?

I support a Community of Practice for one of my consulting clients. The audience includes evaluators who get funding through a very specific CDC program. The total audience size hovers around 200 people. There is no expectation that our audience is going to grow, at least not considerably.

I have emails for what is likely 90% of the potential audience. Meaning I don't have to worry about growing the audience. I can focus directly on communication products designed to serve existing audience members.

Now let's look at the audience I try to reach through my blog and other personal digital projects. My primary goal is to serve the global evaluation community.

To guess the total number we can look at the size of different evaluation professional organizations and LinkedIn group memberships. We can also estimate based on the number of large nonprofits, NGOs, Universities, and government programs that likely have evaluators working within. It's going to be a hard number to pin down, but it's at least 100,000 and likely much higher.

My professional email list at the moment includes around 3,000 emails, many of the people on this list are evaluators. But even if I assume that I reach 2,000 evaluators, that's out of a low estimate of 100,000 global evaluators. So I'm only reaching 2%. That means, if I intend to reach more of that larger audience, I need to work on audience building as well as audience serving.

The way you approach reporting needs to account for the number of people in your potential audience that you currently reach. The higher the saturation the less you need to focus on things like social media.

If you have someone's email, email them. They are much more likely to read that email than see your social media post. If you don't have their email, or know how to find them through other channels, social media offers a potential avenue.

Our new website looks amazing!
Too bad I'm the only one who
knows that it exists.

freshspectrum

Audience Reach Splash Model

Businesses on the web tend to design their communications around a sales funnel. A sales funnel is just a strategy for how you might turn strangers into customers. At the top of the funnel you cast a wide net, then the funnel gets narrower and narrower as you approach the paying customer at the bottom.

Reporting is not selling, it's serving. While you likely have different audiences, there isn't the same kind of hierarchy and flow. It's possible you might want to reach a casual audience because you have information they need to know, not because you are trying to turn them into a higher interest audience. As such, the traditional funnel approach doesn't really apply.

So instead I use what I call a splash model, which is just three concentric circles. The center circle is your high interest audience, the second circle is your medium interest audience, and the outer circle is your low interest/casual audience. Occasionally I'll add a fourth circle to represent the potential audience not yet reached.

I call it a splash model because the goal is to first serve the audience in the middle, and in doing so try to make a big enough splash to reach the others as well.

Let's say you create a big report to serve your highest interest audiences. You might even launch that report with a webinar discussion series with co-authors and partners. This is the rock that triggers the splash.

To make a bigger splash you adapt the big report into smaller executive summaries and infographics. This will push your ideas out towards the medium and casual interest audiences. You can also adapt the webinar recording into short social videos.

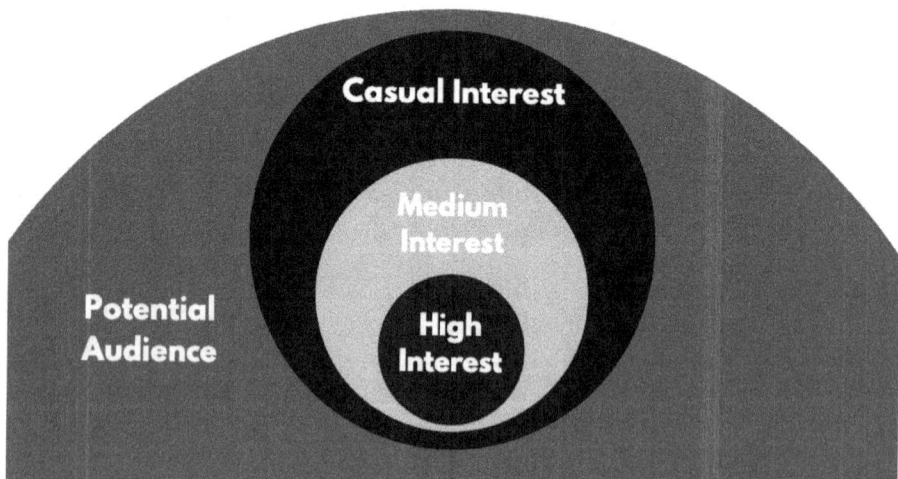

In order to reach all of our diverse audiences, the final report is now 17,000 pages.

You can pick it up here. hand-trucks are available at the back of the room.

freshspectrum

Measuring Your Audience

Now that we have the theory out of the way, let's make everything a little more measurable. In order to define our digital audience in a way that we can count, let's use a few imperfect proxies.

- We will consider your highest interest audience as all the people who have willingly shared their email address with you.

- Your medium interest audience had at one time or another clicked a follow button on Twitter, a like button on Facebook, a subscribe button on YouTube, or whatever else they needed to do to follow you on another channel.

- Your casual interest audience includes all the people who visit your website and see your social content, but don't follow you directly.

- And finally, your potential audience includes the overall number of people you estimate might be considered part of your audience.

So starting from the center of the model we have:

- **High Interest Audience:** Number of people on your email list.
- **Medium Interest Audience:** Number of people who follow you on social media (across all active channels)
- **Casual Audience:** Social Media Impressions (followers across all active social channels) + Website Visitors (unique visitors).
- **Potential Audience:** Estimate this. If you were to serve every single person in your audience, this would be the total number served.

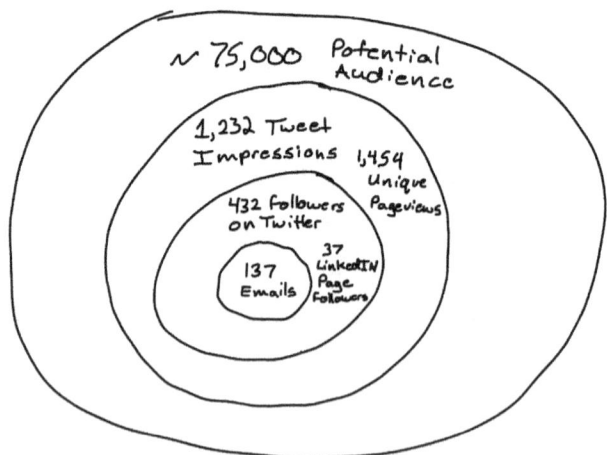

This report reads like it was written just for me.

That's because it was.

freshspectrum.com

Audience Building or Serving?

Generally it takes more work to build an audience than to serve an audience. But not all of the content you create needs to help you build your audience. Like I mentioned previously, if you are already reaching a high percentage of your potential audience you don't have to put much effort into audience building. And even if that's not the case, sometimes just serving the audience you currently reach is enough.

But if you do want to build your audience, how you go about it depends on which audience you would like to build.

- **High Interest Audience:** To grow this audience you need to create the kind of content that someone would be willing to give you their email address to get. Content in this category might include digital summits, webinars, eBooks, toolkits, online communities, eCourses, whitepapers, and, occasionally, long PDF reports.

- **Medium Interest Audience:** Growing a social media following is less about individual content or events and more about providing consistent value over time. Audience building at this level is a marathon, not a sprint. Focus on writing regular blog posts, posting consistently, and engaging potential audience members in digital conversations.

- **Casual Audience:** With social media you reach other audience's by having other people or organization's share your work. You can do this intentionally through direct collaboration, strategic mentions, hashtags, and viral content. You can also grow your website's reach through search engine optimization (SEO) and well-designed content strategy.

As for serving an audience, just focus on delivering a variety of content based on the audience's interest level. Also, try to reduce friction as much as possible. When you are not building an audience, don't worry about collecting email addresses and try not to create something so complicated that it makes it harder for the audience to access.

Chapter 3
Developing Your Modern Reporting Strategy

Rule #1 - Everyone is overwhelmed.

You have access to lots of information. Not only do you have the world at your fingertips, you also have constant buzzing, dinging, flashing, beeping, and ringing. Our devices are like 3 year olds that never nap, they're constantly yelling, "LOOK AT ME! LOOK AT ME!"

And it's not as though we didn't have other things on our mind. You know, things like family, work, love, and loss.

In our modern digital world you have to assume that the person you are trying to reach is at least a little distracted, and at most, completely overwhelmed. It's not an ideal situation. And no matter how important your message is to your audience, it's still going to be hard for them to see or hear.

So how do you effectively report to a distracted audience?

- Do you try to lure them in with interesting stories and illustrations?
- DO YOU SHOUT?
- Do you just keep talking, hoping someone will listen?
- Do you wait to be noticed?
- Do you try once and then give up?
- Do you ask for help from someone they might trust?

There isn't one easy answer. No single magic strategy that will always work for everyone. Your goal is to find something that might work for you and your audience. At least some of the time.

Activity: The Overwhelmed Reader

Find a report, it could be one you wrote. If you don't have a report handy, just check your favorite nonprofit, government agency, or NGO and download one from their reports page. Don't read it yet, just download it.

Now it's time to do some acting.

Pretend that you're super busy and that you have a lot on your mind (this will not be a hard role to play). Now pretend someone just sent you this report and asked you to give it a quick read.

Now open up the report and give it a 5 minute read.

Unless you downloaded a super short report, you can't possibly read it all in 5 minutes. So what did you read, and how did you read? Did you just read the headers, look at the pictures, get stuck on a chart, read the intro, read the conclusion, or just skim through bits and pieces throughout.

This is likely how the bulk of your audience sees your work.

Any takeaways or lessons learned for the next time you go to create a report?

The Old Way to Report

The old reporting strategy used by many organizations is a resource library filled with PDFs. Every time a new report gets created, a new download page gets added to the library. Dissemination is then left to the organization's communications team (or person).

It's possible the research or evaluation team might schedule a briefing or two with important stakeholders. Their direct clients will also receive a copy of the report (often in advance with opportunities to provide edits). The research or evaluation team might also present findings at relevant conferences.

This is not really a strategy. It's more a collection of reporting habits developed over decades. It may be sufficient to help you reach your high interest audience. Whether or not you reach your medium interest audience depends on the additional activities you undertake after publishing the report (i.e. conference talks, briefings, webinars, etc.). Whether or not you reach your casual interest audience depends almost entirely on how much your communications team shares your work.

The biggest problem I've seen is that after publishing the research and evaluation team quickly gives up ownership of the report. It's written, so it is now in the hands of their client or their communication's team.

While there are some amazing comms teams out in the world, they are not the ones who know the most about that report's purpose, content, and audience. Plus, they have other priorities beyond your report. This is why so many reports simply get added to a repository then simply fade away.

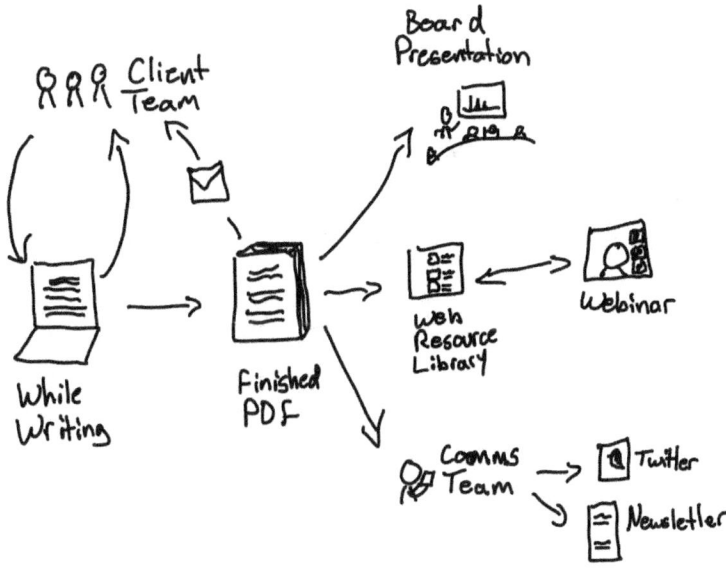

Activity: What is Your Organization's Reporting Strategy?

Think about a report you've written or helped to write.

How was that report shared?

Think about all the people who were given access to the report and how they were given that access. Your goal is to think through the different ways your reports have been shared in the past. Here are some prompts to help:

- Were some of your target audience members involved in helping to write the report? Meaning they would have seen the report at different stages as it was developed.

- Who was emailed directly with an attachment or link to the report? Was this a newsletter sent to an email list or just through individual emails with specific recipients?

- Were there any presentations or webinars delivered to key stakeholders?

- Was the report shared to a website page where a person can then find and download the report?

- Did anyone share the report on social media? Was it shared by a communication's team or just shared by individual members of the research and evaluation team?

- Was there a press release that was released along with the report?

- Were pieces of the report shared in articles or blog posts either on the organization's website or on other organization's websites?

After you're done defining all the ways in which the report was shared, draw a little process diagram showing how all the different pieces fit together over time. Mark which of your big three audiences each piece would have likely reached.

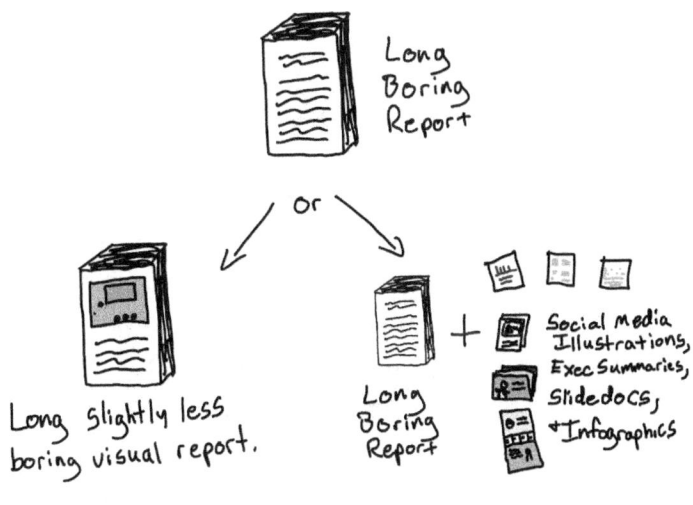

Long Boring Report

or

Long slightly less boring visual report.

Long Boring Report

+ Social Media Illustrations, Exec Summaries, Slidedocs, +Infographics

freshspectrum

Towards a Practical Strategy.

Reporting should be easy.

Do you really have trouble talking about your work with other people?

Over time we've taken the simple act of sharing what we're doing (and what we're learning) and turned it into one big boring document.

I'm going to give you just three different strategies. In the first edition I shared six strategies! It was overkill. After working with my own report design clients over the past few years, I know from experience that you can make any of these three work.

The Modern PDF Strategy is a simple update to the old way. I don't think it goes far enough, but it might be an improvement to the way you report right now. It's also the easiest change to make in slow-moving organizations.

The Web Report Strategy is essentially the digital equivalent to the old way. Simply switching from PDF-First to HTML-First can make a HUGE difference in terms of reach.

The Report Blogging Strategy is my favorite but it does require a change in mindset (product to process). That said, it's ultimately easier, cheaper, and, I believe, far more effective.

1 Pager

3 Pager

25 Pager

The Modern PDF Strategy

I mentioned the 1:3:25 approach earlier in the book when talking about your 3 big audiences. It isn't a new or modern strategy but if you are currently only creating and sharing one long PDF report it would be an improvement.

The 25 page report should be written with your highest interest audience in mind. The 3 page executive summary (or summaries) should be designed for your medium interest audiences. The one pagers are designed to really quickly share specific points or connect with specific members of your overall casual audience.

Most of the organizations that follow this strategy still default to PDF but might treat their reports like a bundled product.

I'm writing another book at the moment that I'm calling tentatively, "The PDF Must Die." So if you're wondering how I really feel, that's it. That said, you can still make some usability improvements even if you do still default to a PDF.

- Try landscape instead of profile (a.k.a. slide doc style).
- Improve the graphic design.
- Systematically illustrate.
- Improve the readability.
- Create some (non-PDF) digital products alongside your one-pagers & executive summaries.

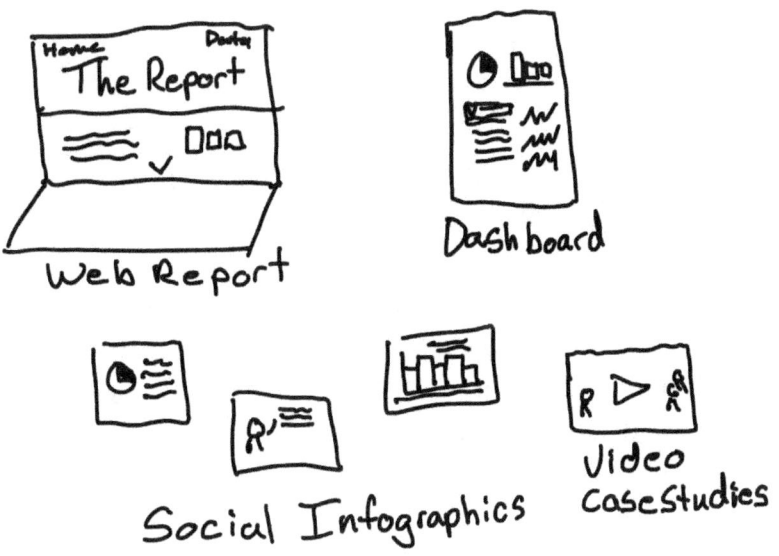

Web Report

Dashboard

Social Infographics

Video Case Studies

The Web Report Strategy

I've seen this strategy being taken by several large NGOs. In a lot of ways it's just a digital version of The Modern PDF Strategy.

Your big report (in place of the 25 pager) is a website report. It might include a downloadable PDF as well, but that's secondary.

The report is written like a good website resource page, with good copy and lots of images. A data dashboard and other supporting content might also be made available through direct links from the main web report.

To help expand the distribution of the report there are often associated webinars or presentations, each linking back to the main web report. Internal organization influencers (such as an organization director or research lead) might also provide video overviews talking about specific aspects of the report.

Along with the web report you also find a supporting social media strategy. This might include social media infographics, videos, and coordinated hashtag use by the organization and a variety of stakeholders or audience influencers.

The web report strategy is less about over-time continuous reporting and more about making a big splash. It turns a simple report release into a virtual cross-platform event.

The Report Blogging Strategy

This strategy mimics modern digital marketing strategies.

Instead of a report, you have a blog (or an email newsletter). You write and share posts or emails when you have something to share.

A lot of our report content is known well before the end of an evaluation or research project. So in your posts you can talk through your goals, share your evaluation or research questions, and talk about your methods.

This strategy can really help you develop an audience, build a relationship with that audience, and get feedback that could influence future decisions.

Whether you center your strategy around a blog or email newsletter, there are lots of options, even if you have zero budget. WordPress.com, Substack, and Medium are all free, well known, and easy to use.

You will also have far better analytics than any PDF centered approach. From email open and click rates to page views and search engine stats, there is a lot you can learn about what's working and what's not.

You can also open up comments on a blog or ask for replies with an email newsletter.

Dissemination (The Sharing Part)

The three strategies I shared will guide the development of your reporting products. But just because you create a nice report, it doesn't mean that report will fall into the hands of your readers.

Perhaps your organization has a really good comms team. But even if that's true, I think it's important for the people who know the content to play an active role in sharing the content.

And if you don't have a clue about social media or audience building, no worries. I'll give you a few simple dissemination tips to help you get going.

In the rest of the chapter I'll show you.

- A simple audience borrowing approach for when you don't have one.
- How to build a basic content calendar.
- How to use webinars to amplify your audience building.
- Why sometimes the best way to share your report is to teach your report.

And just know. If you find something that else works well in helping you to share data with your audiences, just do more of that. Trust yourself because you're also a human being.

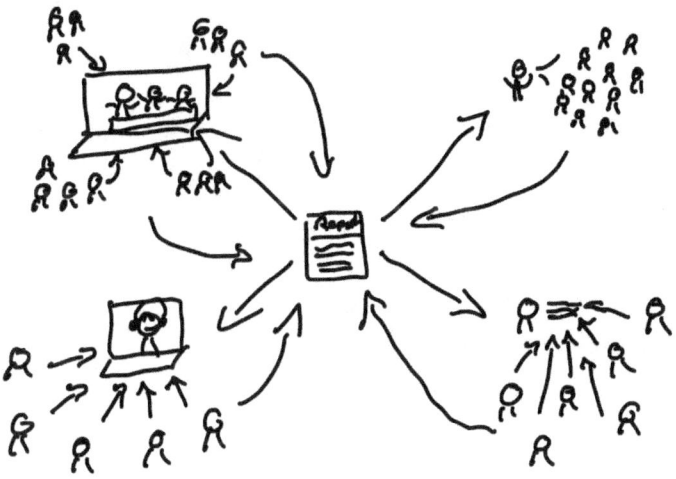

Audience Borrowing

You may not have direct access to your audience and it can take a lot of time to build one. But if others already have a connection with the people you want to reach, you may be able to borrow access.

Bloggers and podcasters who are just getting started often face the no audience challenge. On the web a guest blog posting strategy, or simply volunteering to be a podcast guest, is one of the quickest ways to reach an audience before you've built one of your own. We can do the same with our reporting.

Start by looking for the influencers that currently reach the audience you would like to reach, then collaborate. There are all sorts of ways to collaborate that could be in both of your best interests.

- Virtual summits bringing together different community influencers.
- Panel webinars and Q&As.
- Guest blogs.
- Coordinated social media posts.
- Joining a relevant podcast as a guest.
- Sponsoring digital content.

One tip, start by reaching out to existing connections. Cold emails asking for favors are not often that effective. If you do not know someone directly, try to find a common connection.

You also want to make sure you have a way to collect emails from people interested in following your reporting. This could be as simple as a landing page describing your work and offering a chance to join your newsletter.

Using a Content Calendar

If you already have emails for the majority of your target audiences, there is no need for any kind of expansive social media or blogging strategy. Just email them.

Social media marketers are already know the power of an email list. But so many research and evaluation teams undervalue their current reach.

Start with your own email list and then drip your report out over time. Set a pace for your newsletters (weekly, biweekly, monthly, bimonthly, etc.) and stick to it. Share what you have to share when you have it ready. Keeping pace means creating internal deadlines that can help keep you on track.

Most email newsletter services also allow you to share a public html version for each email. This gives you something to share when an audience member comes late to your email list, or when you would like to reference a past newsletter.

1 Slidedoc
3 Blog Posts
25 Social Media Posts
we suggest using a modern 1:3:25 reporting strategy.
freshspectrum

Webinar Sharing

Human beings are funny creatures. Over the years I made a discovery. It's easier to get a person to register and attend a 60 minute webinar than it is to get a person to read a PDF report for 20 minutes.

By sharing your report with a webinar series you claim space and time in your audience's calendars to present your work and answer questions.

Advertising the webinar on social media, creating the webinar registration page, and connecting with your attendees before and after the webinar creates opportunities to share infographics and other reporting sound bytes. You can also adapt your webinar recordings into smaller length videos to share through YouTube.

Webinars are really useful for audience building as registering with an email address is expected and follow-up (with recordings and future webinar offerings) is often appreciated.

freshspectrum

Teach Your Report

Trying to enhance organizational learning. Perhaps you have been evaluating the effectiveness of a model program. Or maybe you are undertaking a type of formative or developmental evaluation.

Why not turn all of your lessons learned into learning objectives. Then build it into an online learning community.

A good learning community will often mix self-paced modules, live office hours or Q&A sessions, webinar presentations, discussion groups, forums, and downloadable resources.

Think about it, offering a free course or learning community just feels more valuable compared to a regular report.

Chapter 4
Leading the
Change

Why spend time talking to potential report readers when we can sit around a board room table asking what if questions and pretending we already know the answers.

freshspectrum

The HiPPO Problem

If you have ever written or designed anything for a client or a boss, you have likely run into the HiPPO problem.

What is the HiPPO problem you ask?

HiPPO - Acronym
Highest
Paid
Person's
Opinion

Far too many individuals and organizations let the HiPPO play a key role in their design process. Not intentionally, more because they lack any kind of systematic decision making process. So the person with the biggest paycheck ends up calling the shots.

The problem is that the person who makes the most money...

- is not likely the person with the most design expertise.
- is not likely the person who knows the most about the target audience.
- is not likely heavily involved in most of the initial decision making process.

This isn't to say that your boss' opinion or your client's opinion should not matter. It's just that it shouldn't be the driving force behind your design process.

The easiest way to reduce the HiPPO problem is by establishing a design process that externalizes some of the decisions and leverages design assets.

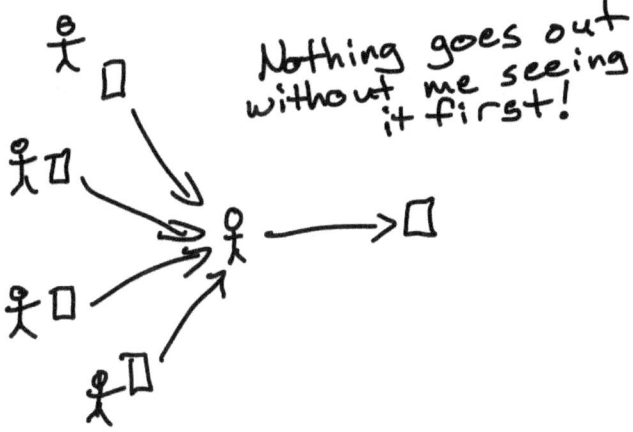

Activity: Finding the HiPPO

Before moving forward, it's a good idea to identify the HiPPOs in your organization. Potential HiPPOs might come from your boss, your client, your boss' boss, or a high paid consultant. The HiPPO might even be your opinion.

We can find the potential HiPPOs with a simple question.

Who in your organization has the power to kill or upend your project with a glance and a word?

For example if this person said, "I don't like this color," you would need to change all the colors. Or perhaps they said, "I don't like scatter plots," and you would be scrambling to change that scatter plot to something else.

Write down the list of people who have that level of authority. These are people you need to factor into your design process.

With enough time and energy I can make an interactive PowerPoint report almost as good as a mediocre website from the late 90s.

freshspectrum

Developing your Design Process

I have a basic 5 step design process that I like to follow for everything from infographics to websites to long reports. These steps are set up to be iterative and you can user test or solicit feedback in between each step.

Step 1. Design Brief: Before you design, write a few sentences about what you hope to design. What is your overall design challenge? What would you consider a successful design?

Step 2. Audience Personas: Who are you designing for? Real people have quirks, so create a few basic profiles of individual audience members. They should be somewhat representative of your target audience. Give them descriptive names (Sally the Project Officer, Dwayne the Board Member, Daria the Volunteer, etc.). Now ask what would each one need or expect from your design? What questions would they ask? Would they even read your report? Which of the big three audiences do they belong to?

Step 3. Mood board: A mood board is useful for laying out your overall vision. In this step you want to collect all the materials you need to create your design including fonts, logos, and colors. You can also include concept sketches, inspirational examples, and any templates or assets you might plan on using.

Step 4. Prototype: A prototype is where you show that you can pull off your vision. It could just be a first draft, or it could be a partial draft showing how the design would look using real software tools. The prototype should be tangible and give any internal partners a practical example of what you had in mind.

Step 5. Final Product: The final product is the goal. It's always possible you will need a few iterations and copy editing passes before you get to the true final product. But hopefully the other pieces of the design process will make this part go faster.

No need showing me any examples. I'll just wait till you put in all the work. Then if I don't like it, you can just start over.

freshspectrum

Reducing HiPPO Problems

To reduce potential HiPPO problems try to get your decision makers involved with the design early in the process.

If you can get sign-off on the design brief there is less of a chance that your HiPPOs will significantly alter the project scope later in the process.

Audience personas can help change the internal conversation. It should never be your opinion versus the HiPPO, unless you are the HiPPO that's an argument you will almost always lose. The persona can help you to shift attention away from opinions towards individual audience member needs.

One of the reasons to use mood boards is to get feedback on visual and technical direction before putting work into the design. This step can also save you from last minute color or font change requests.

The faster that you can create a prototype the better. Our imaginations hardly ever perfectly align and some people will need to see something tangible before understanding your vision.

It is much easier to make big sweeping changes to your designs early in the process, before you have written/coded/formatted everything. If you keep your potential HiPPOs in the loop throughout there is less of a chance that their comments will require a redesign.

The Status Quo Problem.

"It is what it is…"

I hate that phrase. There are processes and protocols that are tough to change, especially in big bureaucratic government, NGO, and nonprofit organizations. But most things can be changed. And not changing them is a choice.

"This is the way it's always been done," is just another form of "it is what it is." It's an excuse we use because it's almost always easier to stick to the status quo. But easier is definitely not always better.

The people who run up against the status quo problem are the kind of people who would read a book titled, "The Reporting Revolution."

Change is hard to bring, and it can take some time. But here is a quick approach you can use to introduce creative work in status quo following organizations. It's called double delivering.

The Power of Double Delivering

Double delivering is just what it sounds like. Instead of delivering one version of a design, you deliver two. For the first you create something basic (i.e. the status quo way). For the second, you try something creative.

I know it sounds like extra work (and it probably will be extra work) but if you really want to push creative boundaries inside of conservative organizations, a little bit of extra work is almost a necessity. And even if you have support to try something new, I still suggest you create two options.

If you bring a new design to your boss and ask if they like it, they might say yes or they might say no. If no, you go back and redesign, then you bring it back to your boss for another thumbs up, thumbs down conversation. This can turn into an endless feedback cycle and get really annoying, it can also cause you to miss deadlines.

When you offer two alternatives you change the conversation because which one do you prefer is a very different question. It forces a choice. They might go for the boring version or the creative version. But they are far less likely to send you all the way back to the drawing board.

freshspectrum

Choosing your Reporting Software Stack

Your reporting needs will NEVER be solved with just one tool. Regardless of any promises made to you by software companies. In the IT world technical needs are often met with a software stack, not a single tool. It's best to think of your reporting needs in that same way.

This is not to stop you from experimenting with different tools, but it's good to have an idea of your usual reporting software stack. Let's first look at traditional reporting software.

What software tool do you use...

- to analyze your data? (i.e. SPSS, SAS, R, Google Sheets, and Excel)
- to create your charts? (i.e. Excel, Google Sheets, PowerPoint, R, and Adobe Illustrator)
- to write your reports? (i.e. Word, Google Docs, and Pages)
- to design your reports? (i.e. Publisher and InDesign)
- to create your slide decks? (i.e. PowerPoint, Keynote, and Google Slides)
- to develop your data dashboards? (i.e. Tableau, PowerBI, and Google Data Studio)

Many organizations leave the choices up to individuals and teams. I think that is a good idea, but when planning out potential templates and training guides, having specific suggested software can be incredibly helpful.

I'll stick with Excel, thank you very much. All those other programs don't let you create the snazzy 3D pie charts everyone loves.

freshspectrum

Your Modern Reporting Software Stack

Now let's look at some of your modern reporting software. What software tool do you use...

- to develop websites? (i.e. Wordpress, Drupal, SquareSpace, and Wix)
- to create social media featured images? (i.e. Canva and PowerPoint)
- to capture screen recordings? (i.e. Loom, Descript, Windows Game Bar, and QuickTime)
- to deliver webinars? (i.e. Zoom, GoToMeeting, YouTube Live, and Microsoft Teams)

- to produce explainer videos? (i.e. Canva, PowToon, and Vyond)
- to edit video? (i.e. Adobe Premiere, iMovie, Camtasia, and Screenflow)
- to monitor social media? (i.e. Hootsuite, Buffer, and Sprout Social)
- to deliver email newsletters? (i.e. MailChimp, ConstantContact, and Convertkit)
- to build an online community? (i.e Circle, BuddyPress, Slack, and Discord)
- to develop interactive charts? (i.e. Flourish, Datawrapper, and Tableau)
- to develop eLearning modules? (i.e. Teachable, Thinkific, Wordpress, and Articulate 360)

In each of the above examples I only offered a few examples of common software, there are many more tools to choose from. There are also other areas I did not cover.

Even though it might be overwhelming, remember, it's always better to think through the options when you have the time rather than right before the project deadline.

Creating a Simple Style Guide

Not only can a style guide help you to "stay on brand" it can also reduce some of the decision burden you face later in the reporting process.

One of the lessons I have learned time and time again is that even if a group is not tied to any specific branding guidelines, it is worth the time and effort to create a simple style guide. The last thing you want to do with a quickly approaching deadline is have a conversation about colors, fonts, and logos.

At the bare minimum, here is what you should include in your simple style guide.

- All relevant logo files needed for inclusion in your report.
- A basic color palette.
- Fonts for headings, subheadings, and body text.

Try to create your style guide as early as possible. It can take time to get the relevant logo files and updated branding guidance when it exists. Early is also the time to decide on colors and fonts.

By using filler text like lorem ipsum, you can design before you have the words.

Report Writing, Report Design, and Report Illustration are Three Different Steps

One thing that slows down report writing is the feeling that you need to design and illustrate your report as you write your report. Countless hours get wasted by data people reformatting tables or assembling figures in Word only to have those tables and figures scrapped later and redesigned using other tools.

I am someone who regularly writes, designs, and illustrates reports for a living. But I do not do all three tasks at the same time. Here is my usual process.

I write in a Google Doc. The only formatting I do during the writing stage is to apply heading styles. My report writing process usually starts with just an outline of basic headings covering all the information I plan to include in my report. Then I write underneath each individual heading.

Lately I spend most of my time designing reports using Canva. I will often build a report shell in tandem with the Google Doc. Most of the time a report can be designed before it is written by using placeholder text. The design step can also help to inform your writing by giving you target word counts based on the placeholder text for each section of the report. You can also use placeholder images for future illustration.

The illustration step happens in tandem with the writing or following the writing. Some illustrations, such as stock images, can be used to set a tone or provide spacing for the words to do their work. Other illustrations, like charts, figures, drawings, and photographs, can become critically important features that can sometimes tell the story of your work better than the words. These types of illustrations might also influence the writing.

It's only after the words are all written, the report template is approved, and the illustrations are reviewed that I bring everything together into a single report.

This is a nice 200 page comprehensive report.

Now can you cut it down to 2 pages? Maybe just take away the methods, evidence and findings?

Developing an Asset Library

Building a personal asset library can help you create reports faster. Modern visual reports of any style use a lot of images from stock photos to icons. Your library doesn't have to be anything fancy, it could just be a folder on your personal desktop, on a shared server, or in a repository like Dropbox.

Just like any other asset, digital assets are accumulated over time. Your job is to be on the lookout for things that could be useful for future reports. Here are some of the things I would include in your asset library.

Charts and Graphs: If you create a chart you like, save a copy of the file where you created the chart. Then name the file according to the assets you have inside. So if you created a really nice stacked bar chart in Excel, save the file inside your library as "Stacked Bar Chart," this will make it far easier to search for in the future. If you used private data, intentionally corrupt and de-identify the data before saving it into your asset library.

Icons: There are lots of good and inexpensive royalty free icon libraries on the web. A lot of the icons we choose are really specific to the context of our work and our sense of style. Just because you found an icon once doesn't mean you'll find it again, so save the icons you use into your asset library. Just make sure to check the site you downloaded them from to ensure that reuse is still within your rights.

Photos: Stock photos can be really useful, just follow the same advice as I gave with the Icons. But most of the time you also have a really powerful camera in your pocket, use it. You may not be able to take photographs of people for privacy reasons, but you can still take pictures of related objects and locations. Also keep an eye out for relevant photographs taken by others.

Example Reports: So far I have mentioned usable assets, but keeping an inspiration folder is also a good idea. If you really liked the style of someone else's report, save it to your inspiration folder. Sometimes inspiration will be a website or link. In those situations I suggest taking a screenshot and saving it inside a document with a direct link back to the website.

I prefer to
Create all my
reports from scratch.
Templates make it
all too easy.

freshspectrum

Building out Templates

Many modern design software products are anchored by a large library of design templates. The templates become the first thing you see when you open up the program. In older software, templates were more of an afterthought. The idea being that you want to start with a blank slate.

The reason for the shift is simple. Templates make design faster, as tweaking a template to make it your own is much easier than starting from scratch. They can also result in better design, as a lot of the design questions have already been answered by someone with ample design experience.

With design tools like Canva and Flourish, you can also save any design as a template link that someone else can click on and use. But you can also create a template in any program by just saving a copy of a file and putting it into a template folder. I realize that many tools have specialty template file types but I often find them a little clunky and just prefer having a copy of the original file.

When intentionally building out templates, use placeholder text, placeholder images, and placeholder charts. The placeholder content should be easy to spot in a simple copy edit so it does not accidentally end up in a published version of a report.

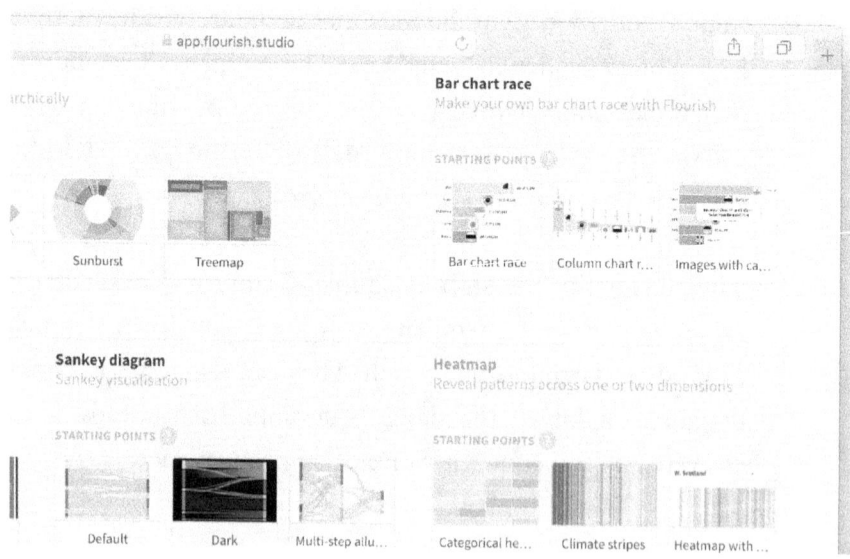

So there is no style guide, format requirements, content requests, or other additional guidance. Just keep it short?

One quick follow-up, does anyone actually give a shit?

freshspectrum

Chapter 5
A Call to Action

If Not You, Then Who?

Lots of organizations settle for the same long, boring, ugly reports year after year after year.

They have convinced themselves that they don't have the money, time, or talent to do better. And you know what? They don't.

But YOU do. The real secret behind better modern reports isn't fancy software or massive design budgets. It's simply a person who really cares.

Someone who looks at bad reports and thinks "we can do better." And is willing to put in the work to make better happen.

Take Action.

Even if it's just a baby step.

Create one infographic nobody asked you to create. Draw one picture inspired by something you read in a report and share it on social media. Think about one person who you think might value information found in a report you've written, then reach out to them and ask to have a short video chat about the subject.

Stop waiting for someone else to take the lead.

You can take the lead.

I believe in you.

Want More?

Join us at **freshspectrum.com** and you'll get the weekly newsletter trusted by thousands of evaluators worldwide. You'll be the first to hear about upcoming books, new evaluation guides, practical tutorials, upcoming webinars, downloadable resources, and new comics that make evaluation more accessible.

Need help implementing a modern reporting strategy for your organization?

Visit my web report design agency website at **ReportPress.net** and sign up for a free consultation.